HSC

The Animal Kingdom

ENDANGERED ANIMAL

Malcolm Penny

Illustrated by Wendy Meadway

The Bookwright Press
New York · 1988

The Animal Kingdom

Animal Camouflage
Animal Defenses
Animal Evolution
Animal Homes
Animal Migration
Animal Movement
Animal Reproduction
Animals and their Young
Endangered Animals
The Food Chain
Hunting and Stalking

First published in the
United States in 1988 by
The Bookwright Press
387 Park Avenue South
New York, NY 10016

First published in 1988 by
Wayland (Publishers) Ltd
61 Western Road, Hove
East Sussex BN3 1JD, England

© Copyright 1988 Wayland (Publishers) Limited

Library of Congress Cataloging-in-Publication Data

Penny, Malcolm.
    Endangered animals/by Malcolm Penny.
        p.   cm.—(The Animal kingdom)
    Bibliography: p.
    Includes index.
Summary: Discusses the reasons some animals have
become extinct, the current factors which may lead to
extinction of more species, and possible solutions.
    ISBN 0–531–18194–4
    1.   Wildlife   conservation—Juvenile   literature.   2.
Endangered   species—Juvenile   literature.   [1.   Rare
animals.   2.   Extinction   (Biology)   3.   Wildlife
conservation.]   I.   Title.   II.   Series: Penny,   Malcolm.
Animal kingdom.
QL83.P46 1988   87–32452
591'.042–dc19   CIP
                                                       AC

Typeset by DP Press, Sevenoaks, Kent, England
Printed by Casterman SA, Belgium

Words printed in **bold** in the text are
explained in the glossary on page 30.

Contents

Why are animals endangered?

The giant panda, emblem of the World Wildlife Fund, is a familiar example of an endangered animal. It is at risk because the bamboo forests, which it needs for food, are being cut down to create large areas of farmland.

For millions of years, some animals have been dying out and other **species** have been appearing. The animals that died out, like the dinosaurs, may have done so because of sudden changes in the world's climate, or because other species appeared that could hunt them or beat them in the competition for food.

About   years ago, a new **species** appeared that has made life very difficult for all the other animals, as well as for the plants that many of them use for food or shelter. That new species is called *Homo sapiens*, or the human being.

Shoebills, or whale-headed storks, are a threatened species of East Africa. They are in danger because the swamps where they live are being drained to create grazing land for cattle.

Humans have caused four main kinds of danger: they have changed or destroyed the plant life of huge areas of the world, leaving many animals with nowhere to live; they have **polluted** the world with soot, chemicals and oil; they have moved **predators** into countries where the local animals have no defence against them; and they have hunted animals for food, for their skins, or for sport, until some species have become rare or have died out.

When the last one of its kind has died, a species is said to have become extinct. This means that it will never be seen again. The last dodo was killed on Mauritius in 1681, the last great auk in Newfoundland, Canada, in 1844, and the last passenger pigeon in the USA in 1914.

The word 'endangered' is used to describe animals that survive only in very small numbers and may soon become extinct. By the end of this book you will see that many animals all over the world are in great danger. We must act soon to save them.

The falling forests

Over hundreds of years, people have had to cut down forests to make space in which to live, and grow food. Huge areas of Europe and North America were once covered with forests, but they were almost completely cleared. Many animals, such as wolves and bears, became rare as a result.

In the last thirty years tree felling has taken place on a vast scale in the tropical rain forests of South America, Africa and Southeast Asia. Today, about half of these forests have been cleared, to supply lumber to other countries and to provide space for homes and crops. The tropical rain forests are ancient places. Once the huge trees are felled, it will take centuries for them to grow again.

The woolly monkey is perfectly suited to life in the trees of the South American rain forest. However, because of the rapid destruction of their environment and because they are taken from the wild to be sold as pets, woolly monkeys are becoming rare.

Millions of animals of an amazing variety live in the rain forests. For example, the island of Madagascar is the only home of all the species of lemurs. As their rain forest homes are destroyed, these lovely creatures become endangered. In nearby Africa, mountain gorillas now survive only in special reserves set aside for them, as do the orangutans of Southeast Asia. The woolly spider monkey and the tapir are two South American animals also threatened by rain forest destruction, but there are many more.

In China, the giant panda is in great danger because its food supply is decreasing as the mountain forests are cut down. It lives on the leaves and shoots of bamboo. Sometimes all the bamboo plants of an area produce flowers and die. When this happened in the past, the pandas used to move to another area to find bamboo that was still alive. Today the pandas cannot roam so far to find food.

The crested ibis in Japan lost its breeding places when the pine forests where it nested were cut down for firewood. Now there are only eight of these birds left on one small island in Japan.

All of the twenty-one species of lemurs are found only on the island of Madagascar. Pictured here is a ruffed lemur, an endangered species.

The threat from farming

Human beings often have to drain marshes in order to produce land where they can live. Every time a marsh is drained, many wild animals are made homeless. Large birds such as cranes need marshes where they can rest and feed during their long **migration**. Small animals, such as frogs and dragonflies, also depend on wetlands.

Grasslands, too, provide a home for many small animals. In most parts of the world, grass supports snakes, grasshoppers, butterflies, rabbits and mice. Australian grasslands are home to small wallabies, while those of Canada and the United States are inhabited by prairie dogs.

Illustrated here are a bearded tit on a reed, a hunting marsh harrier, a dragonfly, a water vole, a marsh frog and an orange tip butterfly. When marshes are drained to grow crops, creatures like these are made homeless.

Grasslands change when farmers plow them up to plant crops. Instead of supporting many different kinds of wild grasses and flowers, the land is used to grow only one type of plant, such as corn or cotton. The farmers call the unwanted wild plants "weeds," and kill them with strong chemicals. To the little animals, however, the weeds were important for food and shelter.

Sometimes, one species of animal will live and breed in a field where its favorite crop grows, for example, aphids in corn, or weevils among cotton. The farmers call them pests and spray them with poisons called **pesticides** to protect their crops.

If the poisoned insects are eaten by **rodents**, and the rodents are eaten in turn by birds of prey, the poison passes up the **food chain**, where it can cause great damage. Some of the pesticides were banned because of this, but not before they had harmed large numbers of eagles and falcons. Eating prey that contained pesticides caused the birds to lay eggs with very thin shells, which broke before the young could hatch. Happily, in places where the chemicals are no longer used, the numbers of birds of prey are slowly recovering.

Barn owls were once a common sight all over the world. Today they have become rarer, as many of the barns where they nested have been destroyed.

9

Poison in the sea

When people first began to cross the oceans, they used rowing boats or sailing ships. The seabirds and fish were safe because the sea was clean. Even when steam ships were invented, they burned coal or wood and caused no harm to the sea.

The first real danger to sea creatures came earlier this century, when huge tankers appeared on the seas to transport oil from one country to another. When these vast ships collide with obstacles, their oil cargoes may be spilled. Now lumps of black oil can be found on every beach in the world, washed up from some accident at sea, or even from a place where it was deliberately released into the water.

The first sea animals to suffer are the birds. The oil clogs their feathers, so that they can neither fly nor keep warm. When they try to preen themselves, they swallow the oil and are poisoned.

Next, the oil poisons the tiny animals in the **plankton**, which is the main diet of many fish. People become affected when their fish supply runs out or poisons them when they eat it. Oil spills affect albatrosses in the Antarctic and penguins in Patagonia, the southern part of South America. These birds feed on krill (a kind of shrimp), squid and small fish, which are poisoned by oil. When this happens, the penguins, albatrosses, seals and sea lions and even huge whales go hungry because of the oil **pollution**.

Oil is not the only substance that pollutes the ocean. There are other chemicals that are even more poisonous. PCBs are strong chemicals used to make paint. When they were spilled into the ocean, they caused the death of large numbers of puffins on both sides of the North Atlantic Ocean, off the coasts of Europe and Canada.

Living in a polluted world

The land and the air are often more polluted than the sea. Factory chimneys release harmful smoke, which may be blown over countries far away from the place where the pollution was caused.

The smoke from factory chimneys often contains a gas called sulphur dioxide. When mixed with water vapor in the clouds, it forms an **acid**, which falls to the ground next time it rains. If the acid rain lands on limestone country, it is **neutralized** by the limestone, which is an **alkali**. If acid rain falls on granite rock, it remains acid.

Where streams flow over granite rocks, they become acid when acid rain falls into them. In Canada and Scandinavia, such streams are the breeding places for large numbers of salmon and

trout. Not only the fish die but so do many trees near the rivers. This affects birds and insects that use the trees as homes.

When an accident occurs at a chemical factory or a nuclear power station, harmful chemicals or **radiation** may be released into the **environment**. At Seveso in Italy and Bhopal in India, chemical fumes poured into the atmosphere, killing people and many animals after disastrous explosions.

In 1986 the nuclear power station at Chernobyl in the Soviet Union caught fire, leaking radiation into the air, which spread across Europe. In areas where it rained during the radiation leak, radioactive particles were washed into the ground. This has harmed reindeer in Lapland and sheep in Britain that have eaten plants affected by the radiation. It may take many years for the **radioactivity** in the soil, and in the bodies of the animals, to fade away.

The smoke from factory chimneys can pollute the air and kill trees. Industrial waste released into rivers pollutes the water and kills fish. Litter is another form of pollution: in this picture a mouse and a duck have been trapped by plastic litter.

Dangerous strangers

Another very serious danger to wild animals occurs when human beings take animals with them when they travel from one part of the world to another. Some of the animals are taken on purpose, for example cattle, cats and dogs. But others travel as unwanted passengers. Rats, mice, sparrows and many kinds of insects have been taken from one country to another as "stowaways" on board the ships of human explorers and settlers.

When such animals arrive in new countries, especially on islands, the native animals are often not able to compete with them for food or defend themselves against their new predators.

Giant tortoises still survive on some of the Galapagos Islands, in spite of competition from goats, dogs, donkeys, pigs and rats, which were introduced in the past. Many baby giant tortoises are hatched in captivity and then taken back to the islands.

The giant tortoises of the Galapagos Islands were threatened when goats were introduced and began eating the plants on which the tortoises depended for survival.

Explorers in the old days of sailing ships used to leave a few goats on any new island that they found, so that sailors who came after them might find milk and meat. The goats have nearly caused a disaster on the Galapagos Islands, off Ecuador in South America. They have eaten all the vegetation that was once the food of the islands' resident giant tortoises. The tortoises had **evolved** without any competition for their food and were unable to survive once the goats ate them out of house and home. Now there are very few tortoises left on some of the islands and they must be carefully protected.

In the Hawaiian Islands, the main trouble came from cats, which were brought in by people as pets. They killed many of the native Hawaiian birds, such as honeycreepers and the nene, or Hawaiian goose. The goose was saved only by being brought to England and bred in **captivity** until some of the islands had been cleared of cats. Now some of the geese have been taken back and released in safety.

The animals illustrated here are rare species of Australia and New Zealand. They are not shown to scale.

Kangaroos, kakapos and kiwis

Australia and New Zealand are very special islands. Situated far from other land, they are the home of many animals that are found nowhere else in the world. When white settlers arrived from Europe about two hundred years ago, bringing their pets and other animals with them, the local Australasian animals were suddenly placed in great danger.

In New Zealand there were no native mammals except for a few bats. The island's birds were not like those of the rest of the world. The flightless kiwi snuffled about in the leaf litter under trees. The kakapo, a parrot that had lost the ability to fly because it had no predators to fly away from, fed on plants or occasionally lizards. These unusual birds faced no threat from predators and no competition for food until rats, cats and dogs arrived with the European settlers.

Leadbeater's possum
(Australia)

Northern hairy-nosed wombat
(Australia)

Thylacine
(Australia)

In Australia, kangaroos and wallabies were the only grazing animals. These native **marsupials** had never had to compete with other animals for food. But suddenly new rivals, such as sheep and cattle, arrived from Europe. The hare wallaby, potoroo (a small, rat-like kangaroo) and many others became very rare as a result.

The first danger to Australian animals came with the arrival of the Aborigines from the islands to the north, about eight thousand years ago. They brought wild dogs called dingoes with them. The dingo soon took the place of Australia's native marsupial wolf, the thylacine, or Tasmanian tiger. About the size of a large, lean dog, this animal had striped fur and a tail like that of a kangaroo. It is thought that the thylacine is now extinct although some people say that it still survives on Tasmania.

Brush-tailed bettong
(Australia)

Kiwi
(New Zealand)

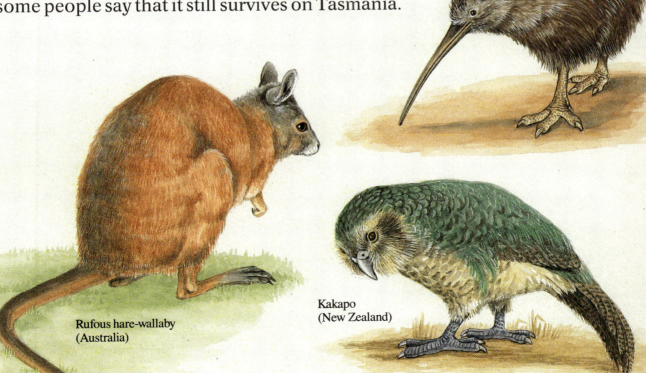

Rufous hare-wallaby
(Australia)

Kakapo
(New Zealand)

The price of beauty

There are many animals in the world that are so beautiful that some people want to capture their beauty for their own use. In the Arctic, seal pups are clubbed to death so that their beautiful soft fur can be used to make expensive coats. Striped and spotted cats have also suffered seriously from the vanity of rich people who want to wear their skins as coats. The South American jaguar and ocelot, the Asian snow leopard and many other cats have become very rare because of this trade, but shamefully they are still hunted.

Fortunately, it is now less fashionable to wear the skins or feathers of wild animals. Birds such as ostriches are no longer killed for their feathers to decorate people's hats. However, large snakes and alligators are still being killed so that their skins can be used to make shoes, belts and handbags.

The jaguar's beautifully patterned coat serves to hide this majestic South American cat in the jungle. Do you think that these rare animals should be killed because some people would like to wear their skins?

Birds kept as pets were usually bred in captivity but sometimes wild ones are trapped and illegally exported to other countries. Illustrated here are the scarlet-chested parrot of Southern Australia (left) and Fischer's lovebird of northern Tanzania (right). Both species are now quite rare in the wild.

There is no need to use the skins of rare animals like these, when farm animals are killed for food every day. Shoes, belts and handbags made from pigskin or cowhide work just as well, and can be made to look just as fashionable as those made from animals that are put in danger by being hunted.

Wild creatures from tropical countries are also traded as pets. Tropical fish such as the colorful cichlids from Lake Malawi in Africa are worth a lot of money. So, too, are parrots and small songbirds from tropical rain forests, and tortoises from North Africa and Madagascar. Many of them die on the long journeys from their homes to pet shops in other countries.

Because of the danger to the animals, many governments have banned the pet trade. However people still manage to smuggle animals such as the South American squirrel monkeys and some parakeets. Fortunately, most pet fish and birds are bred in aquariums or cages to be sold as pets.

The sad story of the wolf

Many centuries ago wolves were common in the forests of Europe. Then farming replaced hunting as the most important way of obtaining meat, and wolves became the enemies of mankind because they sometimes killed farm animals. Soon they were nearly wiped out. They were completely destroyed in Britain where the last wolf was killed in 1743.

A few survive in Spain and Scandinavia, but they are still under attack from people who shoot them whenever they see them. In North America, especially in Alaska and the Canadian forests, wolves are still quite common. However, they face great danger from hunters, even though they live far away from farms. Some people even chase wolves in helicopters and shoot them from the air.

This is done for sport because the hunters enjoy it, but there may be another reason as well. Today people still believe that wolves are fierce and attack humans, although in fact they rarely do so. This fear goes back hundreds of years to the time when Europe was covered with huge forests that people had to cross to travel from town to town. The forests contained plenty of wolves, as well as other wild animals that are now rare, such as wild boars and bears.

Naturally, the people were afraid, and many stories were told about the dangers of the forest. Some of these became children's stories, such as "Red Riding Hood" and "The Three Little Pigs."

Wolves were very rare in Europe by the time people crossed the Atlantic to live in North America, but plenty of the animals lived in the settlers' new homeland. Remembering the stories about the big bad wolf, the settlers began to kill them. Sad to say, they are still doing so today.

Opposite *Wolves are sometimes hunted by helicopter in North America, where they are becoming increasingly rare.*

Saving the tiger

Rangers can keep track of the movements of tigers by fitting them with radio collars.

Opposite *Owing to the success of Project Tiger, these magnificent striped cats have a brighter future than many other endangered species. The number of Bengal tigers has increased from under 2,000 in 1972 to over 4,000 in 1983.*

Tigers live in the jungles and tall grasslands of the Indian subcontinent. Long ago, they very rarely killed either cattle or people. Their main prey was forest animals, such as deer, pigs and monkeys. People gradually took over more and more of the forests where the tigers lived, to make villages and to grow crops. They also killed many of the animals that the tigers needed for food. Soon the tigers were forced to kill cattle and, sometimes, the people who were trying to protect the cattle.

When Europeans arrived in India, tigers were seen as pests and everyone was glad when a tiger was killed. Hunting tigers was dangerous, even with rifles. Sometimes the hunter would ride on an elephant; at other times he would hide in a tree house near a cow or a goat that had been tied up as bait. Many hunters were injured or even killed by tigers. It was considered very brave to go tiger hunting, and soon it became a fashionable sport for those who could afford the time and the money to do it.

Before long, there were very few tigers left for the hunters to shoot, and suddenly people realized that they would soon be extinct. In the early 1970s the World Wildlife Fund launched Project Tiger, a great project to save the remaining tigers. They were protected in National Parks and reserves created by the Indian government.

Safe in these areas, the tigers are increasing in numbers. Many other species, including those that are the tigers' prey, are also thriving in the reserves, where hunting is forbidden. Now the tigers do not need to raid nearby farms for cattle. The only people who see them these days are the reserve rangers and a few lucky visitors.

Rhinos in danger

There are five species of rhinoceroses in the world: the black and the white in Africa, the great one-horned in India and Nepal, the Sumatran in a few parts of Southeast Asia, and the Javan in one tiny National Park in Java, Indonesia. All except the white rhino are in great danger.

The danger comes from hunting, but not for food, nor to protect people's crops. It is to provide horns, and also rhino skin, blood and hoofs to people who want to buy them.

Many people in Eastern countries believe that rhino horn is a strong medicine that can cure all kinds of diseases. They are prepared to pay a lot of money for medicines made from rhino horn, or from other parts of the animal.

In North Yemen, in Arabia, every boy is given a special dagger when he becomes a man. He will keep the dagger all his life, so it is a precious possession. The handles of the very best and most expensive daggers have been made from the horn of the black rhino.

Both these uses of rhino horns make the animals very valuable to anybody who hunts them. Although rhinos are protected in parks and reserves, often by armed guards, **poachers** still risk their lives to try to kill them for their horns.

In the northern part of Africa, there are almost no rhinos left. However, in the great parks of Zimbabwe and South Africa the white rhino is safe, and the surviving black rhinos are carefully protected. The other three species, the Javan, Sumatran and great one-horned, survive only in National Parks in their home countries.

Black rhinoceroses are now quite rare. Even when they are kept in special reserves, rangers cannot always protect them from poachers, who illegally hunt and kill them.

A shameful story

People have hunted whales for a very long time. At first, only a few were killed. Men in small open boats would stay close to the shore, killing the whales with harpoons and spears. The oil, whalebone and meat from the whales were used by the people who killed them. Later, other people wanted to use the oil for lamps and machinery, and the whalebone to make ladies' corsets. An international trade grew up, and whaling became a profitable industry.

At first the hunting was carried on in the old dangerous way, by very brave men in small boats, who towed the whales back to shore to extract the oil. Later, the hunters used fast motor boats with guns that fired exploding harpoons to kill the whales without any danger to themselves. Large factory ships were invented to extract the oil without having to go ashore. Whales were killed by the thousands in every ocean in the world.

A huge sperm whale has been killed and brought into a whaling station. Without people to hunt them, whales like this would normally live for seventy years.

African elephant
up to 9 m (30 ft) long from trunk to tail

Blue whale
up to 30 m (98 ft) long from head to tail

It soon became obvious that whales were becoming rare because of this hunting. The oil and whalebone were no longer needed – people could drill out oil from the ground, and use plastic instead of whalebone. Although most countries gave up whaling, Russia, Japan, Norway, Iceland and Korea still continue this cruel practice.

Now it is possible to sail right across the Antarctic Ocean without ever seeing a whale, where once they were so common that explorers in sailing ships could not avoid bumping into them. Even if all whaling were to stop now, it would be more than a hundred years before the whales recovered their numbers.

Now in some oceans of the world, whales face a new threat. They can become trapped for hours in the huge nylon nets used by some fishing boats. Unable to reach the surface to breathe, the whales drown or die of their injuries.

The illustration compares the size of an African elephant, the largest land mammal, and the blue whale, the largest mammal ever to have lived. It would be tragic if the blue whale, already endangered, were to become extinct.

How can we save our wildlife?

During this century people have begun to realize that many animals will become extinct unless we take care of them. Looking after wild animals and the places where they live is called conservation.

We have already seen how tigers have been saved. Other animals are being protected in all corners of the world, from whooping cranes in North America to small kangaroos in Australia and orangutans in Asia. Where the danger to the animals comes from hunting, they can be protected by laws and by guards to enforce the laws.

Sometimes the animals are so rare that the only hope is to breed them in captivity in zoos until they can be returned to their homes. The Hawaiian goose and the Arabian oryx are two examples. Both are now living safely in the wild once more.

Orangutans of Southeast Asia have declined in numbers over recent years because of the destruction of their forest habitat. Now they survive only in special reserves.

Where the danger comes from the destruction of the animals' **habitat**, for example by clearing forests, draining wetlands, or plowing up grasslands, areas can be set aside to provide some of the animals with homes. The most difficult task is to stop polluting the environment, which harms all kinds of animals. To do this all the countries of the world must work together.

There are many organizations that people can join in order to help save and protect endangered animals and their habitats. Some of them are listed at the back of this book. All of these organizations need our support if there are to be any wild animals and wild places left for our children and grandchildren to enjoy.

An Arabian oryx photographed at Phoenix Zoo, Arizona, where these animals were successfully bred in captivity. They have since been returned to their natural home in Oman and now their numbers are steadily increasing.

Glossary

Acid A chemical substance that eats away at certain metals. It turns blue litmus paper red.

Alkali A chemical substance that may reduce the effect of an acid. It turns red litmus paper blue.

Captivity The condition of being held as a prisoner. A captive animal is kept in an enclosure after it has been taken from the wild.

Environment The world around us, including the air, water and soil and all animals and plants.

Evolved Developed over a long time.

Food chain A natural "chain" which starts with plants that are eaten by small animals, which are eaten by larger animals, which in turn are preyed upon by even larger animals.

Habitat The particular area where an animal or plant lives. Field, river, woodland, mountain and desert are different kinds of habitats.

Marsupials A group of mammals whose females have pouches in which their young develop.

Migration The seasonal movements of groups of animals from one part of the world to another, and back again.

Neutralized Made neutral, that is, neither acid nor alkali.

Pesticides Chemicals sprayed on fields to poison "pests" that attack crops, for example aphids. Unfortunately, pesticides also harm many other animals and have a harmful effect on the environment.

Plankton The mass of tiny plants and animals that drifts in oceans, rivers and lakes.

Poachers People who illegally hunt protected animals.

Polluted Made unclean.

Pollution The condition of the environment when it has been made unclean by factory smoke, chemical spills and litter.

Predators Animals that hunt other animals for food.

Radiation The sending out of rays or particles from a radioactive substance.

Radioactivity The ability of a substance to release harmful radiation. A harmless substance can absorb leaked radiation and then release harmful radiation itself.

Rodent An animal with long teeth used for gnawing. Rats, squirrels, beavers and porcupines are all rodents.

Species A group of animals, different from all other groups, that can breed together to produce young, which can also breed together.

Picture acknowledgments

The publishers would like to thank all those who provided photographs for this book: Bruce Coleman Limited 18 (L.C. Marigo); Oxford Scientific Films 7 (Stouffer Enterprises/Animals Animals), 26 (Tony Martin); Survival Anglia Limited 5 (Cindy Buxton), 6, 14 (Alan Root), 10 (Jeff Foott), 22 (Dieter and Mary Plage), 29 (Jen and Des Bartlett). The photograph on page 9 was taken by Sarah McKenzie.

Further information

To find out more about endangered wildlife and conservation, you may want to read the books listed below.

Animal Ecology by Mark Lambert and John Williams. (The Bookwright Press) Franklin Watts, 1987.

The Answer Book About Animals by Mary Elting. Putnam Publishing Group, 1984.

Endangered Animals by Dean Morris. Raintree Publishers, 1984.

Endangered Animals by Lynn M. Stone. Children's Press, 1982.

Extinct Animals by John Benton. Wonder Books, 1974.

Finding Out About Conservation by John Bentley and Bill Charlton. David and Charles, 1983.

The Future of the Environment by Mark Lambert. (The Bookwright Press) Franklin Watts, 1986.

How Animals Live by Philip Steele. Franklin Watts, 1985.

Hunters and the Hunted: Surviving in the Animal World by Dorothy H. Patent. Holiday, 1981.

Orangutan: Endangered Ape by Aline Amon. Atheneum, 1977.

Prehistoric Mammals by Susanne Miller. Simon and Schuster, 1984.

Save the Earth! An Ecology Handbook for Kids by Betty Miles. Knopf, 1974.

Secrets of Animal Survival by Donald J. Crump, ed. National Geographic, 1983.

Sharing the Kingdom: Animals and Their Rights by Karen O'Connor. Dodd, 1984.

To the Brink of Extinction by Edward Ricciuti. Harper & Row Junior Books, 1974.

There are many organizations that are trying to protect and save endangered animals and their habitats. By joining one of those listed below, you can give your support.

Audubon Naturalist Society of the Central Atlantic States
8940 Jones Mill Road
Chevy Chase, Maryland 20815
301–652–9188

The Conservation Foundation
1717 Massachusetts Avenue, N.W.
Washington D.C. 20036
202–797–4300

Greenpeace USA
1611 Connecticut Avenue, N.W.
Washington D.C. 20009
202–462–1177

The Humane Society of the USA
2100 L Street, N.W.
Washington D.C. 20037
202–452–1100

The International Fund for Animal Welfare
P.O. Box 193
Yarmouth Port, Massachusetts 02675
617–363–4944

National Wildlife Federation
1412 16th Street, N.W.
Washington D.C. 20036
202–797–6800

Index